The Unforgiven Walk Alone

When Forgiveness Isn't an Option

CAROLE SANEK

GWN Publishing, LLC

Disclaimer: This book is a memoir. It reflects the author's present recollections of experiences over time. Some names and characteristics have been changed to protect the privacy of individuals, some events have been compressed, and some dialogue has been recreated.

Published by: GWN Publishing
www.GWNPublishing.com

Cover Design: Kristina Conatser

ISBN: 978-1-965971-13-0

This book is dedicated to YOU.

You are the person I hoped to reach. The one who has been looking for the answer to the question I asked, the one who has been wanting to know the answer locked deep in your heart, you are the one who is looking for peace and healing in a life that deserves to have it.

Contents

Prologue

T RAUMA, as defined by the *American Psycho-logical Association*, is any disturbing experience that results in significant fear, helplessness, dissociation, confusion, or other disruptive feelings intense enough to have long-lasting negative effects on a person's attitudes, behavior, and other aspects of functioning. More information on this can be found in the article: *Guidelines to Incorporate Trauma-Informed Care Strategies in Qualitative Research* by Rebecca Wong.

Most of us will have a significant traumatic event in our lifetime or a series of lesser traumatic events; either way, however, our brain and body reactions will be different, and no one can predict the outcome.

***

As a young child my grandmother would invite me to spend the weekend with her. On nice days we would go downtown and crash a wedding. We had a lovely church on the square of the city, and we would wait until the bride walked down the aisle before we entered the church. I have such fond memories of spending these Saturdays with my grandmother.

I was a teenager with dreams. I would lie on an old quilt under our apple tree in the back-yard and leaf through ladies magazines showing perfect homes with beautiful rooms and lovely gardens. I dreamed of meeting a wonderful man and having a beautiful relationship in which we would spend time falling in love, becoming engaged, marry, and have children. I saw my future as a package with a beautiful red love ribbon.

I daydreamed as I rode the bus to work and home again. I would sit in the bridal salon at our local department store and watch young women try on gowns. You might say, I was in *love* with love.

During the summer I worked as a receptionist at an office's local beverage distribution plant. We needed help and had a temporary agency placement for about a week. Her name was Beverly, and we got to know each other over lunch. One day, Beverly suggested that I come on a blind date with her boyfriend's neighbor that weekend.

This is how I met Donald, the man of my dreams, the love I had been looking for: the marriage, the children, the whole package, or so I believed.

***

We married in 1967. I was pregnant, and we ran away to Michigan, where it was legal to marry at eighteen. My mother slapped me across the face when I told her I had gotten married and was pregnant. After a lot of shouting and crying, I packed my bags and moved in with Donald.

Life went on. I was a young wife and mother when our first son, Adam, was born. We moved forward in our marriage, having our second son, Paul, three years later. We wanted a daughter, and after trying again, our daughter Lexie was born. I was living my dream.

My husband, Donald, worked as a machinist at a large company. He would sometimes travel for work. On the other hand, I was a stay-at-home mom until I decided to finish my education.

Donald worked the second shift because it

paid more, and when offered overtime, he would often stay all night. We did everything families did. We took yearly vacations, giving the kids a glimpse into other parts of our country. We took them to Canada, often staying in Niagara Falls for several nights.

I worked part-time and became fond of making the kids' clothes. I got adventurous and made a lot of my own clothes, too. It was a relaxing hobby as they grew up and were all in school.

Everything appeared to be fine, but everything turned upside down in the autumn of 1979. We had moved to the suburbs by now, and I was working the second shift as a nurse at a local hospital. Donald returned to working days so that I could go to work during the evening/night. The children stayed home with their father and my mother for five evenings every two weeks. I did not sense fear in the air of our home. Looking back, I'm sure this was when everything began to spiral into hell; this was when the worst thing anyone could think of was happening.

The sparks of a flame were beginning to burn into our lives. I did not know about the dangerous things going on while I was at work. This was when Donald single-handedly destroyed our family and shredded that red ribbon to pieces.

Chapter One

The Night the Stars Went Dark

~ 1986 ~

It was late winter. I was sitting on my bed and talking on the phone when Adam entered my room. He stood there and said, "Do you know what I hated most about Dad?"

Hate is such a strong word, and I was surprised to hear him say it. He continued, and his words were ugly and vile, and my worst nightmare had just begun, only it was not a nightmare; there was no waking up from this. My skin prickled, I shook, I trembled, I screamed, I moaned, I beat the mattress, and I cried.

~ 1976 ~

My father passed away in the autumn of 1971, and he had been my rock. When I was pregnant with Paul, he would stop at our house on his way home after work and play with Adam while I napped. Dad and Adam would play on the living room floor with *Sesame Street* on the television, casting the only light in the room. He adored Adam. He took him to softball games in the summer when he was only three.

Eventually, Donald and I knew it was time to leave the inner city and the home Donald had grown up in and move to the suburbs. We were living in what marketing experts called *the ghetto*. Our zip code told retailers we couldn't afford to shop at their stores.

Donald's mother had passed away, leaving us the house. We had no house payment, and while we lived in a poor neighborhood, we were not poor.

We knew it was time to look for a better neighborhood for our children's safety, which eventually became a sick and sad matter. However, it was time to move away from the motorcycle noise, fumes, and the bar fights at the corner bar. Then, there was a bank robbery on the corner, with guns drawn, where I worked as a school crossing guard. It was time to start looking for a safer place to live.

~ 1979 ~

After eight years as a widow, my mother eventually reached a point where she couldn't afford to live by herself any longer. We partnered, and I began to look for homes where we could all live nicely, all while giving her privacy from the noise of three children and a dog. We finally made an offer on a house with an in-law suite, where she had an apartment upstairs.

Negotiations started, and soon, we had our new home. She had her privacy, and we shared dinners every night when I did not work the second shift at the hospital.

Even though our arrangements were tight, we had made it into a lovely home. The house had a big furnished basement and an in-ground swimming pool in the backyard. We purchased a pool table and created an excellent hangout for everyone. The children loved it, as did their friends, and our home became a popular gathering place. I soon fed more than just my family. It was all okay because I liked watching all of them come in and out of our days and evenings. Life was as perfect as I had dreamed it would be.

We could afford everything our children wanted to do. They played baseball and basketball, swam, and participated in scouting and dance classes. We had a dog and, eventually, three cats. Our backyard was an oasis of plants, and a deck surrounded the entire pool. On warm spring days, I would sit outside and express my gratitude for everything we had; I did not know the red ribbon was fraying.

I was sure we had everything I had ever desired. When I was a child, I wanted babies. As I grew older, I wanted love and romance with a perfect man. It felt like everything had fallen into place.

We were an average middle-class family living in the suburbs. I loved to cook, and we had great meals. We also had game nights, and the children played the video games that had just become popular.

I had returned to school to finish my nursing education; everything was as close to perfect as possible. Except it wouldn't last; I had no idea the stars would disappear from the sky and I would face years of total darkness.

Chapter Two

Monsters Only Creep In The Dark

~ 1979 ~

I worked the second shift because the timing worked well for me; mornings were busier, and evenings were not as much. The children came home from school at about 3:15 p.m., and their father got home about an hour later. They were latch-key kids and handled it well. On the other hand, I liked my work and schedule. I was home to see the kids off to school every day, and when I did not work, I was there to hug them and hear about their days. I worked part-time, and it all fit well.

~ 1981 ~

These next two years went by quickly. Nearing Halloween, I pulled a day shift weekend to work because we had planned an adult Halloween party with friends at our house. It was a great Saturday night filled with fun and laughter. The children snuck down to peek at adults in costumes, and the night was filled with great friends and a full liquor cabinet.

I went to work the next day, and before I went to work, I left instructions for my mother to start our dinner. I called home several times to check on everyone, and my mother told me that

Donald was on the couch, not feeling very well. I thought it was probably too much partying the night before. When I came home, I found him still lying down. I took his vital signs, and his blood pressure was shallow. I asked him about his symptoms. It was then that I noticed the bandages on his wrists, and after I asked him about them, he told me that he had taken a handful of Tylenol and had attempted to cut his wrists.

I sat next to him in shock. *How had we gone from a great life to this? How had we hosted a big party the night before and then this? How had he ever thought to attempt to commit suicide. How had that perfect life I had dreamed about, all tied up in a red ribbon, become untied?*

I was so scared, confused, and angry. I started to cry in fear that he could be dying from an overdose.

I was crying and begging him to get up which

he eventually did and all the while I was making phone calls. I called my babysitter to come and get my children, I called the doctors at the hospital where I worked and they told me they would be waiting for us at the Emergency Room. He was put on a psychiatric hold and transferred to a psychiatric facility for three days of evaluation.

During this time, he told his doctors that he had tried three different ways to kill himself; he had even gotten in the bathtub and dropped a transistor radio into the water. However, because none of his actions worked, the professionals called this a cry for help. This was problematic though, because he refused to tell anyone what was troubling him and why he did it. He signed himself out on the third day and came home as if nothing had happened.

I was shocked and tried to keep it from the kids, but they eventually figured it out. My head was a mess, and all I remember is that from that point on, we became the most codependent people on earth. We lived in a terror zone where if we ever upset him, he would try to kill himself again and, this time, die. Our home was ruled by anxiety and fear, and the children suffered greatly.

We were all traumatized. I was supposed to keep everyone safe, keep our lives together, and slap a smile on my face when my husband came home from work. It was torture. We all waited for that other shoe to drop; we just did not know it wasn't a shoe that would eventually drop. It was a nuclear explosion, and we were unprepared for the fall out of it all when our world fell apart.

This was a terrible way to live. I told a therapist years later that the definition of co-dependency was constantly having to make everything so goddamn perfect.

IT WAS EXHAUSTING.
AND FAR FROM PERFECT.

I knew it was time to bring some semblance of normalcy into our lives, and by the following fall, I had found a new position with a new company. I worked daytime hours and was home in the evenings.

The monsters could no longer creep in the dark, but the darkness couldn't hide them either.

Chapter Three

"Fake It Till You Make It" Was Our Motto

~ 1981–1986 ~

T he following five years were frightening for all of us, yet we tried to be that average family with a dog, three cats, my mother, and three children, and living our lives without a playbook.

We did understand his suicide attempts were his cry for help. We became enablers. We lived a life of pretense, always trying to make sure we did not upset him. We were faking our lives. We constantly feared he would do it again, and this is no way to raise children.

I was the one running around, gluing every-thing and everyone together; he was the one tear-ing us all apart. He was cruel; he wouldn't talk to anyone. He would get up and walk away if the children tried to make him laugh. He did this as if being cruel was his way of demanding the respect he knew he had lost from all of us. He was dark and brooding. He walked around head down, never making eye contact with anyone un-less we spoke to him. Every day was sheer hell because we never knew what mood he would be in.

Then, out of nowhere, he became obsessed with creating a beautiful home for us. The house was completely remodeled on the inside as the next two or three summers passed. New grasscloth wallpaper was hung in the living room, and new furniture was purchased. Donald bought a new TV set with all the fancy attachments. The exterior of our home was wholly sided over, not with aluminum siding, oh no, with natural wood panels. The backyard became the perfect place to sit and have peace. All new outdoor furniture was purchased, and the landscaping made the yard look like we were living on an island in the Caribbean. It all made no sense, but we would be at peace more often if he were busy doing something he liked to do. He left everyone alone except to ask for assistance if he worked on projects.

Adam and Paul were teenagers, and Lexie was following close behind. We believed much of what we had gone through was in the past. We planned a fantastic week-long trip to Disney World in 1984. While we were there, I could let go of most of the stress as I watched everyone have a perfect time. We had every meal with the characters, laughed a lot, and the children talked about it for years afterward. And I thought it was just the magic we needed.

Did we hold onto that magic?

No, not really. When we got home, I noticed this underlying current of something being off-tune. I just couldn't put my finger on it. The magic had died when the jet plane turned off its engines at the airport. Now, I look back and realize the magic blew away because we had to return to the real world.

Chapter Four

The Stroke Of Bad Luck Begins

~ 1985 ~

In February, the unimaginable happened. I was awakened by a loud noise in the middle of the night, and I realized half of the bed was empty. I jumped up and tried to open the bathroom door, but it wouldn't budge.

By then, I knew that Donald had fallen and was lying against it, possibly unconscious. I shoved the door with all my might.

When I finally managed to get the door open, I checked him for injuries as best as possible. I moved him into a sitting position on the floor. That was when I realized he had possibly had a stroke. His speech was confusing, and he couldn't answer any questions. I had Donald rushed to the hospital as quickly as I could.

Over the next week, the diagnosis was made that he had had nine strokes. *Nine strokes.* He was in the hospital for two weeks; I spent those days at work and my evenings at the hospital with Donald. My mother and Adam held down the fort, caring for Paul and Lexie and ensuring essential things were done; I did not get much sleep and wasn't eating. In fact, I lost so much weight my clothes did not fit comfortably.

At this time, Paul began to do things that got him in trouble at school. I did not understand why he was acting out. I thought it was because he was frightened about his father. We all knew our lives would change significantly, and we were frightened. This was all new to us. I had stroke patients at work but not at home.

When I brought Donald home from the hospital, the children and I set up sleeping arrangements for him in our family room, and I was his caretaker as he recovered. In recovery, it was discovered he needed to have immediate surgery on his carotid artery as it was becoming dangerously narrowed.

Arrangements were made, surgery was scheduled, and he was admitted to the hospital for this surgery. I drove him to the hospital, and the children left for school. While I was at the hospital and Donald was in surgery, Paul set his school locker on fire. When the police found me, I asked that he be admitted to the same hospital on a psychiatric hold. Something was wrong with Paul; I knew this in my heart, and it was wrecking me.

As their father recovered again, I had to be in court as the decision was coming down on what would happen to Paul. The judge decided that Paul had to be placed in a home for children with issues. This option was much better than putting Paul in a juvenile detention home. Also, this place was close to home.

Our entire family was heading in different directions, and our marriage had been heading downhill ever since Donald's suicide attempts. No one was happy; we were all living under an umbrella of fear. He and I were no longer intimate, and our home was even more tense as he recovered.

The rest of this year was a blur. I had a deteriorating marriage and a child in a *home for trou-*

bled children, and we all had to attend mandatory counseling. The weight of the circumstances often felt unbearable. Looking back, I'm not sure how I stayed sane through the constant attack on my emotional strength.

The strokes had left Donald partially paralyzed on the right side, and his speech was also affected. The muscles on the right side of his face drooped, and all he could do was shake his head yes or no when the therapist asked any questions. The rest of the time, it always looked as if he was grinning at us, and it was a scary and sick look.

The truth is, our family was a mess. The children were not doing well in school. No one was happy.

***

At some point after dinner one night, Donald and I discussed a divorce. We sat across the table, and I touched his hand as he talked. This was a tough decision to make. It was a challenging topic for both of us to talk about. It only added to my confusion about his reasoning, yet I knew it was probably the best decision for the sake of our children.

He had applied for disability. He knew he couldn't work much longer, but his company was keeping him on as a favor. Donald also knew that he was frightening the children; if he had only admitted how much and for how long he had been frightening them, things might have been different.

We agreed to separate and found an apartment for him, and Donald arranged for co-workers to pick him up and bring him back after work. He wasn't allowed to drive. He was on anti-seizure medications from all the strokes he had suffered, and these same strokes had affected his emotions as well as his skills.

Sometimes, he would act like a child and come to the house and get the car keys from one of the children or perhaps my mother. He would show up where I was with my friends and just stare at me. He knew where to find me because the children always knew where I was. I would take the keys away from him and call my son to come to get him and drive him home.

Things began to take a very frightening turn. My life began to unfold as a psychological thriller, and I had no one to turn to for help.

Chapter Five

The Wolves Were At Our Door

~ LATE 1985 ~

Money was tough. Donald was still working. He went with his friends to a local bar to cash their checks on payday. I would drive there to collect the court-ordered child support money personally. I had to do this, or we would not receive any money. It was embarrassing. His co-workers bullied me by making jokes, calling me names, and making obnoxious noises. Still, I continued to go there until the day Donald was told he could no longer work for the company due to the liability to the company for having him work there. After this time, he would bring me his support money every weekend when he visited the children.

I was grateful for some caring and supportive friends in my life. I always had backup, and I often relied on that support network. However, times became more financially tricky, and I frequently had to borrow money from a friend and pay him back in full when I got paid.

My children ate complimentary breakfasts and lunches at school, hot dogs, and mac and cheese for dinner. Our refrigerator/freezer was primarily empty.

I would stop every night after work at the Holiday Inn next to my office building, and for 95 cents, I could have Diet Coke and whatever was available at the happy hour bar for dinner. I ate fried appetizers Monday through Friday, and no lunch. Breakfast was coffee on the go, that was it.

We had taken a second mortgage on the house from all the remodeling we did, which wasn't necessary then, and bills piled high. The child support got us through...barely.

My car was getting older, and the winters were full of road salt from the snow and ice. One day, the tailpipe developed a hole in a rusted spot. I had to crawl on my back, under my car, and wrap it in duct tape. When it came loose, I wrapped it again. This is an example of how we lived...constantly patching the holes in our lives.

Yet we made it. I was running a local office for a national company, still using my nursing skills, and my schedule was not nine-to-five; I could stop home during the day. My friends helped me with the children; they took them to movies or out to dinner to ease the frustration of going from having it all to having almost nothing.

This was a complete 360-degree turn from what I had always believed I would have with that perfect marriage, kids, house, dog, cats, and more. The red ribbon tying the perfect life dream was coming apart. It was a disaster and getting worse.

Then the stalking and terrorizing events began to happen. The telephone would ring, and I could only hear breathing on the other end. I knew it was Donald. It became more terrifying because Donald wasn't afraid to tell me what he was doing. My phone would ring at work, and he would say, "I am in your house. What are you going to do about it?"

I would immediately dial 911 and then drive home as fast as possible. When I arrived at our street, I stopped at the stop sign and saw Donald standing in our bay window. There he stood, a hulking shadow of a man, and I knew he was enjoying this control and torture. I would wait for the police to show up, and when they did, Donald would take off out of a window and be gone.

My expensive jewelry went missing, and some articles of clothing were damaged. I felt nauseated when I thought of him touching my things. I could tell he was going through my dresser drawers. So I packed a suitcase with my undergarments and kept it in my office, re-stocking it when I did my laundry.

Then, everything came to a grand finale for me. Donald called me at work to tell me he was in my house. When the police got there this time, they had their guns drawn. They told me the house was clear, but it wasn't. Paul had cut school and broken into the house like his dad did through a basement window.

When Paul heard his father breaking into the house, he hid under the couch in our basement. Looking back, he might not have endured that experience if he had made a sound.

Before I could file a restraining order, Donald broke in again and destroyed every appliance in our basement: the freezer, the furnace, the washer, and the dryer. It was winter, and we had no heat.

The police ruled this a break-in, and my insurance paid for repairing everything. The restraining order was served, and the courts told him he could only have visitation when I was home. From then on, all visitation was restricted to me having to be there. He could not take the children anywhere.

I lived with more terror in my head and heart because I knew he was outraged. I did not tell the children the lengths their father would go to, in his sickness, to frighten me until months later.

I received notice in December that our divorce would be finalized in January, but finalizing it did not mean the terrorizing would stop; I knew that. Oh no, it was only getting worse. The phone calls kept coming, and I would see him standing across the busy road, staring at our home on days when he did not have visitation.

***

It was early winter 1986. I was talking on the phone while sitting on my bed when Adam entered my room. He stood there and said, "Do you know what I hated most about Dad?"

I looked at him, curious to hear his revelation. Then Adam vomited up words, and five years of agony, anger, and possibly guilt that he had carried all this time became my burden. I was covered in those words, and I understood everything in one stunning moment of revelation.

He hated missing summer vacations because he always had to help his father remodel our home when he wanted to play baseball.

He told me a couple of other things, silly things, and then he said the words that froze me on the spot, **"I ALSO HATED THE NAKED WRESTLING MATCHES."**

IT ALL HIT ME LIKE A TON OF BRICKS.

SUDDENLY, IT ALL MADE SENSE.

I left my bedroom and emptied my stomach's contents into the toilet. I sat on the toilet seat crying, not knowing what to do next. I was left with a bitter taste in my mouth, a splitting headache of anger, and the urge to commit a crime against my ex-husband.

I did not need anyone to translate what those words meant. I knew very well that the man who was supposed to love, cherish and protect his children was a fucking monster. He was a predator. He was a child molester. Donald had manipulated his children into performing sexual acts on him, and if this is making you nauseous, imagine how it made me feel.

From that evening on, our lives were more upside down than ever. Days were filled with horror, embarrassment, shock, anger, and grief.

He had committed an unforgivable act and he was sentenced to walk through life alone. How does anyone ever forgive the unforgivable?

Chapter Six

All Women Are Whores

After I cleaned myself up, I returned to my bedroom and asked Adam if he had been a victim. He told me he hadn't and that his father would ask him to leave the bedroom, but he never told me anything about it. Donald told all our kids that I would divorce him if I knew. Divorce him? I would have left him and taken the children to safety immediately. This was criminal behavior and a police matter.

IT GOT WORSE.

Adam told me his father would slide a dresser in front of their bedroom door so my mother couldn't walk in on them. I was horrified. Our two youngest children were barricaded into a room with bunk beds, and I could just picture their father lying on the lower bunk. I did not ask for details because my heart couldn't take it. This news was shocking and disturbing, yet it finally all made sense. The three suicide attempts, the refusal to say why he tried to kill himself, and so much more.

I sat on the edge of my bed and heard myself repeatedly saying, *"Oh my God, Oh my God."*

When Adam revealed this horror to me, Paul and Lexie played at their friends' houses. I knew I needed to bring them home immediately. I called them back individually. They climbed up on my high bed, and I questioned them as gently as possible. They loved crawling up on the high bed when we needed to talk. They told the same story. I told them they would never have to see their father again, which was almost the truth—and my sincere hope.

As victims of abuse sometimes do, they just returned to what they had been doing as if this was old news and they had built a wall around it all. This happened five to six years earlier and ended when I took a day shift job. They had endured it all this time, terrified that it could all start again.

I slid to my knees onto the floor, sobbing — filled with anger. Donald was scheduled to have a visitation the next day. I had to take control of myself and protect my children from everything now. I knew the proverbial shit was going to hit the fan, and I dialed a friend to come and get my kids on Sunday morning.

I did not sleep a wink that night, and the following day, as I waved goodbye to the two youngest ones, I prepared myself for what was coming. Their father arrived, and I asked him to sit with me in the living room.

He asked, "Where are the children?"

I replied, "Adam is working, and Paul and Lexie are at a friend's house."

He looked surprised and somewhat taken aback. Then I said, "I want to ask you something."

I took a deep breath and asked, "Why did you sexually abuse our children? How could you do this? They were your children, your babies, you held them, you comforted them and now you have destroyed them."

It all came tumbling out of my mouth; Donald sat there, grinning with the lop-sided look on his face that was the residual from his stroke.

I asked him, "Why did you do this?"

He replied, "Because all women are whores."

His response made no sense to me, so I asked him what he meant. Donald answered, "While you were at work at the hospital, you were sleeping with all the doctors."

I looked at him in disbelief, asking how he thought this could happen. I had been working the second shift. There were five of us taking care of 30 patients, and we barely had a chance to sit down. I couldn't make the connection. *If I were sleeping with the doctors, why molest our children?*

Donald shrugged his shoulders, and it took all the strength I had to remain sitting there when I truly wanted to pound him to the ground. My anger had risen from my utter disgust for him. All I saw was a monster. I had to sit on my hands to keep myself from letting my anger get the best of me.

I finally got up and turned my back to him. I told him he would no longer be able to visit the children, that I was redoing the restraining order, and that I was reporting him to the police as soon as he was out of the house. I ordered him to leave immediately and never return.

I am not sure where the courage came from because afterward, all l I could think about was how sick this man was. I also knew that, at any time, he could have become violent.

Donald rose from the chair and started to the door. He turned, looked at me, and said, "I did it because all women are whores." Then he grinned for real. His face was one big shitty smile.

He left. I was shaking like a leaf as I dialed the police.

My head was spinning, but being home alone allowed me time to figure out how this nightmare had evolved. As the pieces started to come together for me, I knew how the abuse happened. I determined how it related to his first failed suicide attempts, which I now understood to be nothing but a way of controlling the children.

Donald wanted the children to believe he would succeed at killing himself the next time, and it would be their fault. This is how this twisted bastard controlled us. All this time, we thought we had to pretend and make everything perfect, and there Donald was, the great pretender, laughing at it all.

"Oh my God, Oh my God," was all I could say. I was in absolute shock. All those years had passed, and this monster had sexually molested his two younger children.

I sat on the floor, hugging my knees as I rocked back and forth in tears, hoping and praying this was all a bad dream. But it wasn't.

Chapter Seven

Hanging By A Thread

The days passed, and none of us spoke of it. *How could we? It was horrifying.* We mustered through with courage and grace and once again lived in a world of pretense, trying to believe everything was normal.

Not long after, our lives became a police matter, and a woman from the Department of Child Services came knocking at our front door.

When I answered, she told me she was there to remove my two youngest children from the home and place them in a safe environment. I started to object loudly.

Adam appeared at my side and ordered her off our property. He told her that *we had a restraining order against their father and that the safest place for the kids, at this time, was at home, with me, among my mother and him.* It was a proud moment for me to see my son take charge.

After this, she left, and I stood there, shaking. We had to handle everything independently, and the system was failing us.

***

Time passed, and one day in mid-winter, I came home from work and saw Lexie holding a shopping bag filled with money. I asked her where she got all the money from, and she told me that her father had given it to her.

I took a deep breath and asked if he had been in the house. She told me he had only knocked at the door and handed her the bag. I pictured

Donald this close to my daughter, violating the restraining order and my sense of security.

Donald was denied visitation. His sickness had taken everything away from him. He had nothing, and the kids and I were hanging on by a thread. The bank wanted me to pay the second mortgage, but I barely had money to cover the first mortgage.

***

Then, early in April, my phone rang at work in the late afternoon. I was ready to leave for home when Adam called to tell me that the Cleveland Police needed to talk with me and that he had given them my number at work. I hung up the phone, and it rang again. This time, it was an officer from the Cleveland Police calling to tell me they had found a body and identified it as my husband. I remember struggling to find a chair to sit down as the news hit me that he had finally succeeded in dying.

I agreed to come to the police station, and while I knew it was death by suicide, the coroner needed to make that ruling. The living spouse is often a suspect, but I was away for the weekend and had proof. I had been at a friend's house, and my mother watched the children. The coroner did rule it a suicide, and now I had another decision to make: *how to do a funeral.*

Again, there was shock, disbelief, anger, and relief. Yes, there was relief that he could no longer hurt or terrify us.

I understood his choice: going to prison meant that other prisoners would know why he was there. A conviction meant all his friends, neighbors, and family would know. Donald couldn't face it, and so he chose suicide.

He took so much from us, but most of all, he took away the children's chance to ask him why he did it. He died, taking his answers with him. That is an unforgivable act and is part of the reason why I wrote this memoir. *How does anyone forgive the unforgivable?*

Chapter Eight

Trauma Mama

After Donald's suicide, the bullying started. People blamed me, saying that I left him when he became disabled. Oh, he was more than physically disabled, but they did not know that. I tried to let their cruel words wash over me.

They did not know that we had decided to divorce together. It wasn't a one-sided choice. We had agreed to divorce when Donald knew he wouldn't recover completely, and he felt it was right.

The children had been avoiding him. He had moved into our basement and was only coming upstairs for dinner. We decided to divorce long before he began to break into the house and terrify me. He had shifted to a better frame of mind when we decided that divorce was the correct thing to do.

But Donald's demons came calling on him and eventually wore him down. He allowed his memories to stare him in the face. He couldn't avoid them. Something had happened to Donald, maybe when he was a child. His childhood was sketchy. The things he did share were not happy memories. His mother had two husbands, and our former neighbors rumored that she also possibly entertained men to put food on the table.

However, now that he was dead, I was told that it was my fault because Donald was sick, and I just left him cold. He was most undoubtedly ill, but they had no idea how sick he indeed had been, And I didn't feel compelled to defend myself and expose the tragic abuse my children had suffered from this man.

***

At the funeral home, a family friend came up to me, telling me that I had a hell lot of nerve being there.

I looked at him and said, "And you had a hell of a lot of nerve helping him buy the gun he used to kill himself with."

I had discussed with the funeral director that he should stand by for moments like this, and this friend was asked to leave.

What mother would ever allow her children to be alone, to face the judgment of others?

The days and weeks following Donald's death were challenging to get through. People did not understand that Donald was sick and that he could have hurt all of us.

His doctor, a friend from my work at the hospital, phoned to ask me how I could have stopped helping him. She angrily told me he had missed an important medical visit, implying it was my fault. She was the one who asked the police to do a welfare check on him, which led to the discovery of his death.

Then she dumped his diagnosis on me. The most recent ultrasound of his carotid arteries showed that he was in danger of having a massive stroke. I asked her if he knew this information, and she told me she had informed him on the phone about a week before he was found dead. He had set up this appointment to talk about what, if anything, could be done, and I doubt if anything could be.

There was a stream of things happening during Donald's final days. We will never know what finally pushed him to take his life. Was it a felony conviction and prison sentence? A potential massive stroke, or was it because he suddenly realized he had indeed lost everything? We would never know.

More importantly, Donald was mentally ill before he ever experienced the strokes that disabled him. He knew how to trip our triggers, and we were always afraid that he would commit suicide. This was his sick control mechanism.

I don't know if the children ever secretly discussed what to do. I don't know if they told their older brother they were afraid of him and did not want to visit him. *Was that why my oldest son told me what happened five to six years ago?*

I asked myself dozens of times why no one had told me until that night. I remember the *your-mother-will-leave-me* story one of them told me. Damn right, I would have done precisely what I did.

I would have had him arrested, and he would have been gone from our lives.

His immediate family refused to believe he had sexually molested his children. Instead, they were accusing my children of being liars. None of them came to the funeral home. It did not take long for his family to disappear. They were in denial, and I never heard from them again.

Chapter Nine

The Sheriff Was Breathing Down My Neck

Everything was a mess. The shock of it all wore off quickly for me. I was numb. But I needed to pull myself together to determine how we could hold onto our house and how we would eat.

When Donald died, the support money was gone, too. I applied to Social Security for the children but knew the process would take months before I would receive the actual benefits.

I worked hard to prevent them from worrying, but with each passing month, another bill went unpaid. I stopped paying the second mortgage because I could not afford it. I remember the amount well—it was $208.00. Such a small amount caused me great concern.

I had started the death claim for his life insurance policy, but that company dragged its feet. I was on the phone with them weekly, and nothing happened. A foreclosure notice came in the mail, and I had a limited amount of time to pay the overdue balance, and there was no way to do that.

In desperation, I called Donald's former employer on a Wednesday, two days before the sheriff would be at our door. Sobbing on the phone, I begged for the life insurance money. I told them we were being evicted Friday at noon. That was when it clicked for this administrator, and I was told that the check would be cut immediately.

I did not sleep for the next two nights. At 11 AM on Friday, my phone rang. It was FedEx making sure I was home to sign for a letter envelope. The driver pulled up a half-hour later. I hugged him in gratitude and jumped in my car to drive to the bank.

At 11:40 AM, I deposited the life insurance check and paid the second mortgage in full.

***

Over the years, when I have told my story to every therapist I have worked with, their response was always the same. First, they had no clue how I ever held us all together, and then they would tell me it was a miracle I was alive.

Life was better for us after that. Fortunately, Donald had not removed me as a beneficiary of 50 percent of the insurance money. Half went to me, and the other half was divided among my three children. I have yet to learn what they did with their money; it is all a foggy memory.

Nobody was happy. The children did their things. Adam was often out with friends, and Paul kept getting into trouble. He took Adam's car on a joy ride, knocked down a neighbor's fence, and turfed their lawn. He was cutting school. He had been discharged from the home after his father died. It was determined the primary threat to Paul's emotional life was gone. I was surprised he had not been sent back to the home for wayward kids. My daughter grew more and more inward.

We had been so good at pretending for years that the pretense continued. It seemed easier to put it behind us because no one wanted to discuss it, so we did just that.

After all this had happened, there was no

such thing as feeling normal or being a typical family. We were left spinning, not knowing where to land when the spinning stopped.

I used my time to visit my brother, Danny. He lived in NYC, and the airfare was cheap from Cleveland to New York, so I flew there often. It was an escape for me.

Danny lived with his partner Thom most of the time, and he also had a small apartment at 38th and 3rd in the city. I had a key, which made it easy for me to catch a flight out in the late afternoon on Friday and fly back home in the late afternoon on Sunday.

When he offered me a key and a weekend escape, I accepted it with deep gratitude. I loved his partner, Thom. They took me to fantastic places, and I felt so fortunate to be able to do so. I traveled about once a month; that was all I needed to make me feel like I could have a life again.

Even though my mother and I never saw eye to eye, she would take care of the kids over the weekend so that I could have a good time, something I had not had in many years.

I would explore the city during the day on Saturday and join Danny and Thom for dinner and a night of feeling I deserved to have this.

I felt like I was the reincarnation of Holly Golightly. It had been years since I had seen "Breakfast At Tiffany's" but when I was in the city I would also stand at the window of Tiffany's without the cigarette holder and stare at the jewelry store windows.

In the fall of 1986, Thom and Danny invited me to come to New York to be the hostess at their invitation-only event of Andy Warhol's Four Reigning Queens. I was thrilled. I rented an evening gown when I got to the city and felt like a Queen, too. Royalty and people who served the queens were in attendance, and then Warhol showed up. He was driven in the most beautiful Bentley I had ever seen, and on his arm was a woman once married to Mick Jagger.

The following spring, I went to New York one more time. Thom had been diagnosed with HIV and was planning to move back to Amsterdam. I knew my brother needed me, and I used my vacation days to help him through the decision he needed help making: should he stay or go with Thom?

It was never that difficult a decision as Danny was soon diagnosed with HIV, and they wanted to spend their last days together.

I made the most of this last trip to the Big Apple. I also shopped till I dropped one afternoon and took a taxi back to Danny's apartment. He told me afterward that he had never seen the doorman come out and help any tenants who lived there, but he came and helped me. I told him I tip well.

While there, my boss called to tell me our company was merging with another similar company. The following week, I would be swamped with clients, making appointment calls, scheduling lunch dates, and scheduling group presentations; my life was about to change, too.

We had a sad, long goodbye; Danny came to the airport with me to spend as much time together as possible before I left, and as I got up to board my flight, we both had tears on our cheeks. I loved my brother deeply. I was frightened for him; I knew his days were numbered, and he asked me to be the one to tell our mother he had HIV. We agreed she should be told in person.

I handled that sad responsibility and watched my mother crumble in despair. No mother wants to have a child die before she does, and this was incomprehensible to her as she was showing signs of cognitive decline.

I made a big decision. Then I made one more. First, I had to find a facility for my mother. With a friend's help, we found an opening at a very nice nursing home, as by now, my mother needed constant care. She had begun to wander, and that frightened me.

Next, I put the house on the market, and it sold quickly.

Adam agreed to care for Paul. Lexie and I left Cleveland and moved to Chicago for what I hoped would be a fresh start and give me what I had been missing all those years: a life.

I put my running shoes on, and we were gone.

***

I look back now and realize that, with all the trauma I had in my life, it was easier to run away than to face it. I continued to run away for years. I lived in a fantasy world where I did not have to tell anyone what had happened to our family. I didn't have to tell anyone my husband at that time had sexually molested my children, attempted suicide, had nine strokes, and finally killed himself. I did not have to say anything about all we had been through.

I did not have to tell the story of being repeatedly bullied, of having to beg for money, or of being entirely in the dark about what had been going on when I worked the second shift.

It was easier that way, and I needed it to be easy. So, I decided to flee, and I ran away.

Chapter Ten

The Big "F" Word: Flee

I did not know what to do. I have been told that people who have had trauma run as a way to regain a sense of control so that they have something more positive to focus on.

Once upon a time, I had a beautiful home. I would walk in and admire it daily. We had worked hard to have many nice things, but things were only things. Worse yet, the thought came to me that this home was not a shelter; it had not protected anyone from danger.

I ran, on and off for years, and boy did I. The following is a list of all the running I did from 1990 to 2020, and it was a lot of miles:

- Chicago, Illinois, to Champaign, Illinois
- Champaign, Illinois to Richmond, Virginia
- Richmond, Virginia, to Chicago, Illinois
- Chicago, Illinois to Richmond, Virginia
- Richmond, Virginia to St. George Island, Florida
- St. George Island, Florida to Costa Rica
- Costa Rica to Detroit, Michigan
- Detroit, Michigan to Chicago, Illinois
- Chicago, Illinois to Munster, Indiana
- Munster, Indiana to Homosassa, Florida
- Homosassa, Florida, to Brooksville, Florida
- Brooksville, Florida to Land O' Lakes, Florida
- Land O' Lakes, FL to Greenville, South Carolina

And done.

I am exhausted writing that list. I ran from my family. I ran from a different cheating man. I ran from breast cancer. I ran from domestic violence.

I kept running for years. There were years of nightmares. I never felt secure. I would see Donald standing across the street at that bus stop. I would see him, catch glimpses of him, panic over this, and run again. Running became a habit. I put on my running shoes, and I ran. No matter where I ran, I would see him. He would be walking alone as the unforgiven do.

And I was left with that question in my head, *could I forget the unforgivable?*

Running Shoes

Book Two Teaser

GWN Publishing, LLC

The Windy City Years

Chicago 1988-1990

The decision to move to Chicago was easy. It was close to Cleveland, and I could return in half a day to see my mother if needed. It was a city I had fallen in love with as a child on family vacations. I told my parents I would live there someday. I wasn't like Danny. He wanted Los Angeles, San Francisco, New York, and various European cities. Not me. I wanted Chicago.

I drove up on a weekend and found a perfect apartment for Lexie, me, and two cats. Next up was figuring out how to make the move. I enlisted the help of friends and family, and we got everything into a U-Haul van, towed my car, and arrived. The school year wasn't over yet, so I allowed Lexie to go home with a friend and finish her school year before starting high school in Chicago in the fall.

Left alone to my own devices for several months, I worked on the apartment, helped the cats acclimate to their new home, and returned to work.

***

In August, I went home to bring Lexie back with me. As we drove into the city, I chose Lake Shore Drive so she could see its magnificence. Lexie was enrolled in a unique program at a high school on the city's north side, where it was almost like going to college. She now had to use public transportation to get back and forth to school, and she adapted quickly to living in a city filled with people worldwide. However, Lexie always had street smarts, and I knew she would always be okay.

I soon had some lovely friends and great neighbors with interesting jobs, and Lexie had freedom. The apartment I chose for us had a private entry in the back, which gave her freedom that she never abused.

We often spent part of our weekends getting to know the city and even walked downtown on lovely days. If Lexie ever felt lost, I would tell her to look for the Sears Tower so she would know how to walk to get home.

Chicago downtown was about 4 ½ miles from where we lived. We were in a great location. Movies were filmed in the area, and TV shows were written about the area known as Uptown. It was very diverse, and yes, it did have its problems. Still, once we closed our doors, we had a slice of a certain amount of glamor and safety, except for the night the front door of the building was stolen. There was also the incident when robbers broke into our landlord's unit, and he was home. A fight began, and the robber was knocked out of the bathroom window, fell to the first floor, and was trapped in that space. The police removed him by going through the basement. The bathroom window served no real purpose because walls enclosed that open area.

Lexie worked at the local grocery store and was eventually hired by a city country club. The members often hired her to babysit their children, and she was paid well. I had been hired to work for a cancer center and was back treating patients again.

I had to train for this new position in Los Angeles, and I spent two weeks there learning how to use a device designed to kill cancer tumors by heating them to a specific temperature with microwave technology. No patients were ever injured, as a physicist created the dosing of the microwaved areas and then programmed them into the device I was trained to use. I had friends looking in on Lexie; she had her friends now and her work.

***

Our second year began with Lexie being a senior in high school, and I was sent to a conference in Las Vegas, where I became the victim of a theft. I was walking through the casino to the meeting rooms when I was knocked to the ground, and my purse was stolen.

Now I had no ID, no credit cards, no cash, and of all the dumb things I could have done, I left my keys in my purse instead of putting them in the safe in my room.

The hotel graciously had Amex send me a new card from their local office. While I did not put my keys in the hotel safe, I had put some cash in there. My purse was later found in a trash can with my ID intact but no keys.

I called home and had my landlord change our locks, and I started calling the man I had been in a relationship with, who was working in Macon, GA. I knew he had one of my car keys, and I had arranged with an airline to bring my keys to O'Hare if he would just take the key there. I tried to reach him for 3 days, and he never answered. Finally, in desperation, I spoke with the hotel manager in Macon, who told me that while the room was rented in the name of his company, it had never been used. *Well*...

The hotel finally reached him, and while he still had time to take the key to the airport, he didn't drop it off till I was home. I guess that since I busted him, he just didn't care.

***

While at the conference, I met a man who owned a company that manufactured ultrasound hyperthermia devices to treat cancer. Over dinner one night, he asked me if I would like to be the company's Clinical Application Specialist, and I said I would without hesitation.

The only glitch was that this company was two hours away from Chicago, and we would have to move. It all worked out perfectly. Lexie was ready for a change; she graduated in June, and we moved in July.

What a party we had when she graduated. My brother, my mother, and Adam came to celebrate with us, and we had such a great time in this city where I could sometimes see healing beginning to happen, or so I thought.

However, if I had known this would be the last time I would ever see my brother, I would have convinced him to stay longer and play in the windy city. I just never thought he would have less than two years left to live, and dammit, he wasn't supposed to leave me with Mom and without him to grow older with as planned.

My father, the children's father, now my brother, and all the men I had in my life left me to fight the good fight of life alone.

Acknowledgments

When I finally plunged into the deep waters of writing this memoir—about a period in my life that remains painful to this day—I took a deep breath, held my nose, and dived in, peeling back the many layers of my life that I had kept almost secret for over 40 years.

Some of my friends knew fragments of the nine years that shattered my family.

Thank you to those of you who listened to these pieces and parts.

Next, I want to thank all the therapists who have heard my story over the years—there have been many. I am confident I wouldn't be alive today without their support and how they helped keep my head above water.

Special thanks go to Sue Publicover, who edited this manuscript for me. She did an incredible job navigating her wilderness of grief, yet she still found the time to read, edit, and return the manuscript to me with care and dedication.

Finally, I want to thank the seven beta readers who reviewed this story and shared their thoughts with me. Their words—"You are the strongest woman I know," "Your courage amazes me," "The pain you endured grew your resilience," "You are a superwoman," and "This is a compelling and captivating story of forgiveness"—were profound. Some even said, "It was gut-wrenching and brave," and simply, "I cried."

Thank you, dear ones; you helped in so many ways!

Now ask me if I regret anything; I will tell

you, "No because I cannot change anything."

This book recounts an event that unfolded over a long period—9 years, to be exact—and has taken 45 years to put into words. My late husband often encouraged me to write my story, but when he died suddenly in my arms, everything leading up to the moment of writing this memoir was buried in my mind as grief consumed my world.

I am also the author of "Fractured—Living with Grief," a love story memoir intertwined with advice for coping when someone you love dies suddenly. The book is available on Amazon.com.

Greenville, South Carolina, is my home with my dog, Rosie. In addition to being an author, please listen to my daily podcast on life coaching topics. I can be found on most social media platforms, where I strive to inspire and uplift people daily.

You can reach me at:

carolelynnesanek@gmail.com

You can also listen to my podcast here:

https://thrivelive.podbean.com/

About the Author

Carole Sanek

 Carole Sanek is a life coach, podcaster, and author. Carole decided to create a series of memoirs based on a significant trauma in her life that turned her entire world upside down. She spent over forty years turning it right-side up again. Carole spends her time with her dog companion Rosie, walking in the mountains of North and South Carolina.